Building a Boat:

Building a Boat:

Lessons of a 30-year project

Paul Marshall

ISBN: 151537789X
ISBN 13: 9781515377894
Library of Congress Control Number: 2015914634
CreateSpace Independent Publishing Platform
North Charleston, South Carolina

To Susan
with gratitude for all you
have brought into my life

TABLE OF CONTENTS

ACKNOWLEDGEMENTS

Thanks to the Writing Lab. You have been supporters, able listeners and honest responders to the many drafts of this book. Special thanks to Bethany Reid who has guided the writing group for these many years and helped me turn a rough journal into a memoir.

And of course, William Stefon, William Aldridge and the many other able guides, seafaring writers and adventurers who inspired me to leave home. Finally, thanks to my Grandson Sam who asked the questions that launched a boat.

PROLOGUE

"Grampa, what is that thing hanging up there?"
"A boat I've been building for a long time," I said.
"Why don't you bring it down and work on it?"

The damp gray days of November require a fire in my shop. The clean burning, easy to light stove that warms me as I work on my boat hadn't been invented when this story began. Sometimes it feels as if *I* hadn't been invented when this story began.

I look back over the years and my shoulders bend into the hand planes blade. Paper-thin translucent shavings curl off the well-seasoned cedar plank. Bought when I started the boat building journey, this plank has travelled with me through this decades long story.

Four decades have seasoned the board to a rich brown.

The decades show on me, too. My skin has paled and age spots now show in between the thinning stubble of my silver hair. Three wives, countless friends gone, dead or half forgotten. A career started and finished, yet the unfinished boat remains. The boat, such as it is, recently lowered from its place hanging from the ceiling, now holds a place of pride nuzzled in between the chop saw, the wood stove and table saw.

I begin to write this tale in a small paper bound notebook, a compass rose on the cover. I'm surprised by the quirky way the story wants to be told. Writing about my life, like boat building projects, emerges one step after another regardless of what the blue print dictates. Essentially it is an American tale, a story of optimism, romantic intentions and self-determination. I've learned, however, not to trust my judgment about such things. Maybe it is just a story of an everyday man living his life.

BUILDING A BOAT, STEP #1: WHY BUILD A BOAT?

"A boat is a hole in the water into which you pour money."
AUTHOR UNKNOWN

I didn't have a clue what I was doing when this project began. I was, after all, a blue collar kid born of practical, hard laboring parents, land locked and with no boating history. It all seems like a dream now, but impossible as it seems in 2015, the fear and paranoia of the 1970's was reasoned and practical. The "red peril," the "communist threat," the imminent threat of nuclear winter, made it seem possible, even likely, that nuclear bombs would rain down on the Washington State trinity: Ft Lewis, Boeing and the shipyards of Bremerton and Seattle. Back then, as I worried about a post apocalyptic Puget Sound, my choice of a counseling career seemed useless, even self-indulgent. Why, I mused, would anyone worry about self-esteem when just surviving a nuclear disaster filled their days? The question of what to do after the big one fell launched a discussion that started the building of the boat.

My old friend William and I, known for our romantic and catastrophe filled conversations, wondered, earnestly, how one would negotiate the rubble and wreckage of the Seattle area freeway system after the "big one." Any attempt to connect with family and friends from south Puget Sound, would be all but impossible. Of course the solution was as obvious as any map of northwest Washington could make it. Water.

A boat was the perfect solution to transportation and career needs during a crisis. Skilled hands, able to manipulate hand tools could turn good wood into useful objects. The accuracy of this truism ran deep in my family history and nagged to be acknowledged by my college-corrupted mind. The only skills bought along with my college degrees, of much use in a post apocalyptic world, were the ability to read and analyze information, and an inner faith in acquiring solutions from people, books, and experience.

BUILDING A BOAT, STEP #2: HAVE A PLAN.

"The Yankee Tender:
A capacious, seaworthy, flat-bottomed
skiff weighing less than 150 lbs."
THE WOODEN BOAT STORE

On a crisp winter day in 1976 the blue prints for the Yankee Tender arrived in a large cardboard mailing tube. The step-by-step instructions and illustrations promised to help me build a boat. I sat in the yellow and green kitchen, muffled street sounds of Willamette Avenue in the background, the plan drawings drooping over the edges of the breakfast nook table, my eyes darting wildly across each page. Covered with the Prussian blue ink of draftsman's drawings, the pages offered images, measurements, and compound angles enough to cover six pages and fuel my dreams. Words like transom, stem, chine, thwarts, quarter knees and breast hooks baffled me and shook my self-confidence even as they excited my imagination.

In an attempt to regain some sense of perspective, I began an inventory of what I knew and the resources I possessed. A paltry list, but not one of a rank beginner. Perhaps my single most important resource was an optimistic and imaginative spirit.

My mother, before she died, liked to tell the story of "the little rocking chair." My parents had spent money they didn't have, to buy a small hardwood rocker for their young son Paul. In a fit of religious fervor, fueled by Sunday mornings at the Assembly of God church with my Aunt Maryellen and Uncle Ernie, I had become possessed, according to my Mom, with the notion to crucify the cat. I saw that "Old Rugged Cross" cleverly hidden in the legs of my rocking chair. I used a hatchet to release the cross from the constraints of the rocking chair's frame, and tried using my persuasive skills to get the cat to let me hang it on the cross.

The threads of my little boy spirit are still present when I imagined turning a pile of boards into a boat. My optimistic spirit certainly helped me begin a project of this complexity knowing I did not possess all of the tools and skill necessary to complete the job. The lasting insight for me in this story comes from the recognition that throughout the turmoil and chaos of the late 60's and 70's I could imagine a future in which I could thrive and manage.

BUILDING A BOAT, STEP #3: FIND A TEACHER.

"The art of teaching is the art of assisting discovery."
–MARK VAN DOREN

I fell in love with the sea about the same time I met my first true adventurer. His name was Bill Stefon. He was a swarthy, dark haired man with a deep resonant voice who had traveled the world before coming to my small, northwest, logging town to teach and tell tales. He enchanted us, encouraging us to consider living a life beyond our known world.

I was a 7th grade student at R.E. Bennet Jr. High School in Chehalis, Washington. The long hallways and shiny linoleum floors echoed with the sounds of heavy brogue shoes and smelled of Butch Wax and hair spray. My hometown was full of loggers, farmers, merchants and mill workers. It had something like eight churches, at least as many taverns and bars. Somewhere around five thousand peacefully conservative souls, give or take a few red-necked rowdies. They were deeply rooted in their families, their work and the Cascade foothills and Chehalis river valley. They were the children of wayfarers but unlike their grand parents they had found a place to settle and build lives. They told stories and had a mythology, but it was one of hard work and stick-to-itiveness.

Some years after I left Chehalis, a group of college students, carrying out a school project, informed us all that Chehalis had more millionaires per capita than any city in America. The stay at home, hard work attitudes had turned out well for them.

Anyway, Mr. Stefon used his booming voice, dark handsome good looks and 30-year-old youthfulness to entice me into World Geography. It was 1961; I was 13 years old and could barely imagine Seattle, let alone Rome. The images he shared of exotic places and strange people, the first hand stories he told us about Istanbul, Rome, and Frankfurt made him an instant hero in my world. I worshiped him. Sitting in Mr. Stefon's classroom I could smell the sea air of the Mediterranean, hear the sounds of unknown languages, and taste foods rich in color and spices deliciously different from the gray hues of the roast beef and potatoes my mother put on the table. He set my mind on fire with his wondrous stories.

Of course, around the same age I had become especially interested in the worlds of wonder I found in my Grandfather's yellow covered National Geographic Magazines. Brown people, eyes unlike those I knew. Mountain peaks spiking so deeply into the blue skies of a distant Tibet. Bare breasted women and men with banana leaf covered penises. Markets full of blood red lamb carcasses and chickens hanging whole for all to see and smell. Images that sprang complete into the new mental spaces Mr. Stefon had opened for me.

A great teacher and a magic carpet magazine inspired dreams and helped to lay the stout foundation of wonder that would hold up my life. The sea became the first room built on this foundation. A room decorated with thoughts of WWII war ships and the majestic clipper ships of the great open passages across the world's oceans.

I have a vivid memory of one of my family's infrequent visits to the northwest coast of Washington. I sat for hours gazing longingly over the white ocean breakers, ears full of the sounds of crashing waves. I stood, eyes wet from the cold wind, straining to catch glimpses of cargo ships rising and falling on Pacific swells. Where were they going? I imagined foreign sailors standing on deck looking back at me. I wanted to believe they wondered about me.

So long ago I cannot remember the how of it, but some act of serendipity brought this poem to the day dreaming adolescent boy.

Sea Fever

John Masefield (1901)

I must go down to the seas again, to the lonely sea and the sky,
And all I ask is a tall ship and a star to steer her by;
And the wheel's kick and the wind's song and the white sail's shaking,
And a grey mist on the sea's face, and a grey dawn breaking,

I must go down to the seas again, for the call of the running tide
Is a wild call and a clear call that may not be denied;
And all I ask is a windy day with the white clouds flying,
And the flung spray and the blown spume, and the sea-gulls crying.

I must go down to the seas again, to the vagrant gypsy life,
To the gull's way and the whale's way where the wind's like a whetted knife;
And all I ask is a merry yarn from a laughing fellow-rover, and quiet sleep and a sweet dream when the long trick's over.

John Masefield's poem put words and rhyme to my young dreams. The sailor of my imagination had dreamed to return to that which I had never experienced but longed to know. Bill Stefon introduced me to the "vagrant gypsy's life." He turned an institutional green classroom into a place where "merry yarns" were told by "laughing fellow rovers." But until Bill Stefon, no one had made me feel like "a laughing fellow rover."

It is not that the loggers and farmers of my childhood were not merry and certainly could laugh, but they held their dreams and adventures closer to home. Crops were tilled, planted and harvested within a tractor drive from the house. Hunting and fishing was readily found in the forests surrounding us. The great tales of Paul Bunyan and Babe the Blue Ox taught us that the mythic journey of our ancestors had succeeded in bringing us to the hills and valleys of the Cascade Mountains. This place, where I was born, embodied the dreams of my family and those around me. But, I wanted more.

Though I was years comprehending it, from that 1960's autumn in the institutional green classroom, my course was set. I longed to be anywhere away from Chehalis, away from the maple tree lined, cracked side walked streets, away from the fast bicycles and back alley shortcuts.

My vagabond friends and I played on north/south main line freight cars, shunted onto rail sidings, fancying ourselves to be hoboes.

The Beach Boys provided a musical inspiration for these hobo day-dreams about California Girls, Dead Man's Curve and "come on a safari with me."

Freedom Riders in Memphis brought heroic justice to blacks and

Pete Seeger told us, "We shall overcome."

I had never met a hobo, a surfer or a black person, but it had not stopped my day dreaming and wondering about others outside my little town.

Tumble forward six years. Broken bones, loves, losses, cars, music, bands, feeling up, freaking out, fears about the draft and being sent to a green jungle called Viet Nam. I had no way to know it but, ready or not, I was becoming a man.

BUILDING A BOAT, STEP #5: JOIN THE NAVY AND RIDE THE WAVES.

"Anchors Aweigh, my boys,
Anchors Aweigh.
Farewell to foreign shores,
We sail at break of day-ay-ay-ay.
Through our last night ashore,
Drink to the foam,
Until we meet once more.
Here's wishing you a happy voyage home."
OFFICIAL SONG OF THE NAVY

After flunking out of college in the spring of 1967, I arrived at my parents' door, embarrassed and unsure of what to do. Within days I found out. President Richard M. Nixon sent me a letter from "a grateful nation" telling me to report for a physical exam that would assess my ability to go war. I knew I would be killed if I allowed the U.S. Army to take me away. Given no choice, like so many young men through the centuries who had been conscripted by Kings, Pirates, Privateers, I was to be used as fodder in another's quest for glory.

I decided, without consultation or support from any adult, that I'd join the U.S. Navy and become part of the Navy Band. Of course, they didn't promise me anything like a place in the Navy Band. They only promised me an audition and I was happy to think of myself as a sailor not a soldier though both decisions were the result of conscription, not choice. It seems trite now but I liked the navy blue uniform, navy bean soup and the possibility of visiting exotic ports of call. Truthfully, I had not a clue what I had been forced to sign on to and had very few scruples about my situation.

Clueless or not, my roving days had begun. And as Dr. Seuss said, "Oh, the Places You'll Go!" San Diego, California (better know to sailors as "Dego"), Norfolk, Virginia ("We're the girls from Norfolk high, We're the girls from Norfolk high. We don't smoke and we don't drink, Norfolk Norfolk Norfolk), San Francisco, California ("Frisco" as sailors had called it since the early days), Cavity City, Philippines (also known as "Sin City"), Hong Kong, Taipei, and a few reconnaissance flights flown over the South China Sea off the coast of Viet Nam.

Masefield's poem doesn't mention the painful loneliness of roving. Why didn't he forewarn us of the ache in the chest caused by endless waiting? Waiting for orders. Wondering if the orders would send me to Viet Nam. Waiting for a letter at mail call. Waiting for Leave and a chance to go home. Waiting for the impossibly distant day when my obligation to military service would end. Masefield's sojourners must have left family and lovers as they went down to their ships. I suspect he knew that Hellos and Goodbyes are forever changed after the Rover is awakened, and he must have known of the undreamed of experiences and shocking encounters to come. Could I give up experiencing the breath taking oppressiveness of hot, humid, tropical air smacking you in the face upon leaving the conditioned air of a plane? Would I give up the sensuous caress of a tropical sea breeze, the sweet taste of a ripe mango picked from dusty roadside trees, juice dripping from lip to chin to chest? In the shadowy escape of these memories I wondered if I should forget the manic, animal-like energy of men, in a war-room, closing on an enemy. The flash bulb recognition that death and destruction was my mission.

One searing afternoon, mid-way through my life as a sailor, I wandered off the paved streets of Manila onto a dusty narrow side street, unsure what I was drawn to or running from. I passed a small, palm thatched hut where an old Filipino man was sitting in the flickering shade of palm trees. He greeted me using his limited English. All I could do was smile and try hard to find some of my limited Tagalag language skills. He invited me through the open door of his palm frond roofed hut. A plain wood table, varnish long ago scrubbed off, sat in the middle of the room. There he prepared a fresh pineapple for us. His sharp machete sliced graceful diagonal cuts along the rows of eyes in the face of the fruit.

He generously discarded the pithy core and, cutting long thin slices, top to bottom, handed me a slice of heaven. Raised on Del Monte canned fruit, I had no idea about the taste or dreamed a scent as thrilling as that long juicy slice of fresh yellow fruit handed to me on a machete blade.

Why the slightly stooped, black haired, nut-brown skinned man had asked the young, thin hipped, pink skinned, blue-eyed kid into his simple one room hut I'll never know for sure. I suspect, I was as exotic to him as he was to me. I thanked him as best I could and returned to the narrow dusty road. The humid air smelled of Bougainvillea, sea air, raw sewage and hot dust. The clacking rustle of palm fronds in the wind carried me away from this vagabond encounter with the mysterious "other" on the edge of Manila Bay. Sadly, this rare moment of generosity also served as a stark counterpoint to what my life had become.

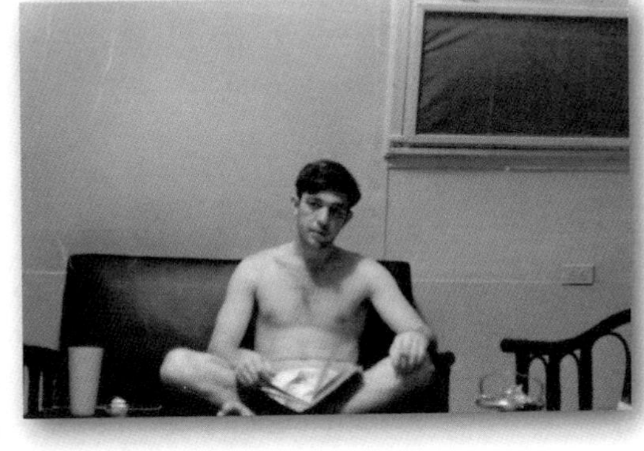

As I remember it now, leaving the dusty side street and reentering the busy Manila street scene I became part of a Felliniesque dream. My world cracked open. Filled with salt sea smells, my mind couldn't hold together the lingering taste of pineapple, hot sun, and noise. The accumulated change from small town boy, to unwitting young warrior, lonely young man adrift in a world of war, drugs, whores, and fear overwhelmed me. A cacophony of senses, thoughts and feelings all merged with the cultural chaos of the 1970's and I was sent spinning into sensory and emotional turmoil.

In this dream, I was walking in the past on the tree-lined sidewalks of my hometown. Surprisingly though, when I looked up, rather than maple trees and two story white houses, I was standing before the doorway of a brightly lit naval command room. Naval officers in white uniforms and gold shoulder bars focused on blowing up a Viet Cong infiltrator trawler. The bright colors and third world urban smells of the scene seemed out of place, but another mental whirlpool brought me onto a Manila street and I was a young boy, wearing dirty bib overalls and a perplexed look. Dazed, I watch brightly colored Jeepnies, hear horns and motorized vehicles of all sorts whizzing by. Waking, my addled mind was lost in confusion and I wondered.

How did I get here? Where is home?

Looking back, it is unsettling to not know how long I stood on that dirty, noisy corner. Four decades make me squirm at the conclusion that the complex emotions of a wartime draft still fill me with an awareness of the divided soul created during those years in service to America. At best, those times, those radically transcendent times, transported me on an unforgettable voyage.

Waving over the next available Jeepnie, I climbed aboard a kaleidoscopic taxi named Big Red, the fighting cock, and found myself speeding back into the flow of traffic on the way to Cavity City. Weathered grey clapboard houses spun by. Brown skinned boys and girls, women and men, old and young, walked, biked and motorbiked along with us. For a moment the changing textures and colors flowed past me like a rushing river made of people, machines and dust. The energetic current pulled me, like it or not, back on course with my strange adventure.

BUILDING A BOAT, STEP #6: A SIDE TRIP WITH JEEPNIES.

"Jeepnies are the most popular means of public transportation in Philippines. They are known for their crowded seating and kitsch decorations, which have become a ubiquitous symbol of Philippine culture and art."

WIKIPEDIA

Please indulge me in a moment's ramble about Filipino Jeepnies.

Transform a WWII jeep by extending the back end by four feet in order to help seat five or six people side by side, backs to the outside, knees bumping slightly, heads brushing the ceiling, and you have an open air, brightly colored Philippine taxi, commonly known as a Jeepnie.

The best part of a Jeepnie, aside from the way it careens down crowded streets with impunity and flair, is its wild paint job. Mad abstract patterns of pinks, golds, greens and reds swirl and curl in hotrod inspired impressions. The eye-popping colors are interspersed with religious sayings professing the saintliness of the driver and the power of the Madonna. The Jeepnie's hood is adorned with Chrome horn bells blasting multi-toned musical tunes that inspire pedestrians, bicyclists and cars to get the hell out of the way, and be quick about it.

A bold person, if fearless, can have the front seat next to the driver to watch through the windshield their doom approach. Doom, in the form of careening cars, trucks, bicycles, motor scooters, pedestrians and more colorful Jeepnie's all crashing toward you, at a heart stopping rate, through a windshield full of family photos, religious icons and tagalog proclamations.

The war was an ever-present background flutter as we careened along the edge of Manila Bay. Even in the amazing taxi it was impossible to escape the uncomfortable possibility of unexpected orders from a distant commander, a distant god who could send you into the feared jungle. A war filled with booby traps, napalm, cluster bomb pockmarked rice paddies and Viet Cong fighters waiting to kill you. Even now I can't effectively describe the effect of this reality. In those days the best I could do was escape into the heavy beat of Carlos Santana, Black Magic Woman. I learned to live with mind altered nights in back alley bars, working 12 hours on/12 hours off shifts at the base radio shack. All the while trying to absorb the television news images of college squares filled with students yelling "Hell no we won't go!" flooding across the Pacific waves to my NAS Sangley Point Quonset hut.

The rainy season was winding down. We were all burned out by the relentless work schedule. The weight of humid air pulled down on us all. I'll never forget the day the Admiral decided to do something about the stress by taking his men on a cruise aboard the base cruiser. A converted WWII mine sweeper, the wood hulled beauty had lots of room in which to entertain Admiral Sandecker and a staff of about 30 officers and enlisted men who helped him command Fleet Air Wing Eight. The Air Wing included two patrol squadrons of P-3 Orion patrol planes, but on this particular day only the admirals direct staff joined him for a booze and BBQ cruise on Manila Bay. The Admiral and his officers stayed inside the main cabin or on the front deck while the enlisted men stayed at the stern drinking beer and listening to music. To our surprise, the Admiral joined "his men" on the fantail.

Drunkenly loud we bellowed out the words to "I feel Like I'm fixin to Die", a Country Joe McDonald anthem for those times.

"Well, it's 1-2-3 what are we fightin' for?
Don't ask me I don't give a damn,
next stop is Viet Nam.

Well, it's 5-6-7 open up the pearly gates.
There ain't no time to wonder why,
Woopie! Wer'e all gonna die."

Followed shortly with Edwin Starr's,

"War, Hunh!
What is it good for?
Absolutely nothing!"

We were drunk and hopeless souls on that boat, filled with despair, anger and the chaos of those times. We weren't even in-country Viet Nam and still we knew the empty feeling of the war. We let it all out. Emboldened by booze and hapless anger, we gave the Admiral, known to us as the Ol' Man, an ear full. He turned and left us without a word. The morale-building cruise was cut short and I only saw the admiral one other time in the year and a half I served the Commander of Fleet Air Wing Eight.

Those four years in the U.S. Navy were unlike any in my life before or after. The "lonely sea and the sky" were my companion to this soul altering period of my life. After decades I can still flashback to it. I am, once again, standing on the breakwater at the edge of the air station runway, late at night, looking east towards home, and watching heat lightning roll across the black Pacific horizon.

BUILDING A BOAT, STEP #7: SO, THE LONG TRICK WAS OVER.

> "The "trick" Masefield is referring to is a "trick at the helm."
> On tall ships, the time one spends steering
> the ship is called a "trick"
> and they often lasted two to four hours.
> At the end of that "long trick" one would
> definitely need a good sleep."
> UNKNOWN BLOG POSTER

Returning home was extremely disorienting. I wanted to return to normal life, but what was normal? I was different from the 19-year-old boy who had left Chehalis four years earlier. The town seemed different, small minded and confining, and the maple trees didn't offer the comforting shade I remembered. A month later I moved away from family to attend college.

It was 1971. Just ten years after meeting Mr. Stefon, I was enrolled in an experimental liberal arts college filled with young, entitled liberals and drop out hippies, one often posing as the other. Not that I was conservative, in fact, the military experience had radicalized me. I now knew that our government lied and did not honor its principles. It was still feeding young fools into the Viet Nam war machine, killing, maiming and crushing spirits. America was not as I had been taught.

Most civilians were not interested in my long trick but a few wanted to hear a tale or two, preferably funny ones, hair raising ones, short ones. Students at The Evergreen State College did not want to hear any of my stories; they were openly hostile to the war and generally uninterested or hostile to veterans. Consequently, I went dark and silent about where I had been for the previous years, and started all over again.

Soon after beginning college I moved in with the girl who had walked the widows walk for me while I was away at war. Her name was Michele and she would become my first wife; it seemed the thing to do. She had a small apartment above a garage on Bliss Beach, a small rocky cove on Eld Inlet. I sat for hours looking out the large living room window that opened onto the inlet, and all the way south to the state capitol dome in Olympia. The view was a long pull for the eye. The grey water and the evergreen tree lined shores was endlessly interesting. I passed time in an old rocking chair, looking at waves and sea birds, drinking beer, reading Hermann Hesse and Fyodor Dostoyevsky, All the while tying to forget my year in service to America.

I had learned to dull pains and doubts with booze and drugs while on my first grand adventure. Those strategies continued to be useful as I changed tack and enrolled in college. While most people I knew bought beer by the bottle or six-pack, I bought it by the case. I could no longer afford to buy amphetamines and pot at the street values of Olympia,

Washington, so I quickly let them go. Alcohol was more affordable but a much more difficult habit to leave behind.

Mr. Stefon had never used his baritone voice and dark good looks to tell us about the identity problems caused by a long sea cruise. William Masefield was capturing a more romantic notion of life at sea; perhaps in his world of gulls and whales, a sailors identity didn't change. Once a sailor, always a sailor. I was no longer the Boy Who Had Gone to Sea. No longer the patriotic boy who would do the right thing and willingly serve his country, but I was still the romantic, wide-eyed traveler. I was still pulled by the promise of adventure and discovery; I was ready to honor Masefield's old ways, if only I could find them in my new world.

The juxtaposition of the beautiful view and my simmering inner demons was a study in crazy opposites. One item was wonderfully out of place in this rocking chair, beer bottle view. She was a 60' long wood hulled tugboat, a perfect balance of form and function. The Sandman had a sweet line and a pert wheelhouse. I imagined myself standing behind her old wooden wheel, pulling log booms around the inlets and harbors of south Puget Sound. I could hear the fog horn and feel the pull of the log rafts trailing astern of the wondrous 70 year old tug.

The war may have jaded my young idealistic views, but every time I looked out across Bliss Beach and saw the old wood boat I knew I was not dead, not dried out and rotting on the beach like a derelict old rowboat. I still dreamed sea-dreams; I still felt the pull of the sea and longed for foreign ports of call.

BUILDING A BOAT, STEP #8: HAVE A FRIEND WHO WILL SUPPORT YOUR COCKAMAMIE IDEAS.

"And talk of poems and prayers and promises and things that we believe in. How sweet it is to love someone, how right it is to care. How long it's been since yesterday and what about tomorrow, what about our dreams and all the memories we share."

JOHN DENVER

It was during these years on Bliss Beach that I began my 40-year friendship with William. It was on Bliss Beach, looking at the peeling blue and gray hull paint of the Sandman that William and I talked of dreams, adventures, social justice and honorable actions. We both thought John Denver's recording of Poems and Prayers and Promises spoke for that time in our lives.

Now, forty years later, I know those conversations added new stones to the life foundation begun years before by Bill Stefon, Admiral Sandecker, and William Masefield.

William and I hatched many crazy ideas about how to make a living with a tugboat. My favorite was the one where we would build a small house on a barge. We would rent it to people and pull them any place they wanted to go. In the midst of tugboat dreams, Willam also helped make real for me the understanding that I was a successful student, and that a graduate degree in counseling was not a senseless daydream. Embedded in those long conversations were the seeds of a conflict that still haunts my life and drives this story forward.

Was I to be a counselor or a boat builder?

A photo, to be found in a box, tucked on some shelf, in some closet, shows me standing (for real not just in my imagination) behind the wheel of the magnificent old tug, The Sandman. Michele had convinced the tug's owner to take us out for an afternoon cruise in celebration of my 24th birthday. "You take the wheel," he said, "I've got some work to do below deck." The cool morning air chilled the hot blush on my face as I stammered out my willingness to take the wheel. There I was, alone at the wheel, the binnacle and compass showed due north, the destination was unclear. His parting comment before going below was, "keep her off the rocks and don't run into other boats in our path."

Bliss Beach, blissful spirit, and a day like none I'd have imagined and not like any since. Tugboats, wood hulls, salt water, and the smell of oil were in my blood.

BUILDING A BOAT, STEP #11: PLAN FOR UNEXPECTED GROUNDINGS.

Breasthook: a V-shaped timber or plate connecting ship timbers or stringers of opposite sides where they run into the stem; also: a similar connecting piece at the stern —called also crutch

MERRIAM WEBSTER DICTIONARY

Bliss Beach, Puget Sound, and tugboat daydreams were lost in the long, wide valley of my graduate school years in Eugene, Oregon. It was impossible to let go of worries in a valley. Troublesome thoughts would roll up the coast range of mountains to the west and roar back down over me and across the valley floor, then up the cascade mountain range to the east and then back again. No endless horizon, no tides sweeping away the mental flotsam and jetsam of life.

I was similarly rolled over by my experiences in a University graduate school program. Far outside of my family roots and working class upbringing, I was similarly off balance in the entire milieu of 1976 Eugene.

You may recall early in this story a mention of the "quirky way this story wants to be told". What may have seemed a long, side trip, to some has in fact been a necessary undergirding for this tale. The story has now returned to itself and I think the two story lines create necessary "stringers" or a "crutch" that helps to hold each other together. The idea of a sort of "Breasthook" for building a boat is the same support necessary to build a life.

Excited as I was to be pursing my dreams as a Psychotherapist, I longed for water, familiar surroundings and the blue-collar sensibilities of my birth. Trips to the Oregon coast helped whet my soul, but it was trips home to the family, and a chance to see Puget Sound and the northwest coast of Washington, that made my shoulders drop and my breath come deep and easy.

The Olympia Tug Boat Races were under way during one of my visits home. I chanced upon a bulletin board announcement about the Wooden Boat Festival in Port Townsend, Washington. Only a month away, the idea of attending the festival pulled at me like mist rising off the sea to a sailor too long ashore. And so, a month later water, boats and wood of all shapes, hues and textures greeted me in the sunny morning air of the old water front boat harbor in Port Townsend. Somewhere in the distance a group of musicians played a lively sea chantey, a large jib sail snapped, filled by a fresh breeze, salty old men sat selling used hand tools. It all wetted my dry parched skin and set my heart free of valley constraints.

A hundred years ago, Port Townsend was a busy port. The sail rigged lumber schooners plied the small dog ports of Puget Sound, gathering lumber bound for California. Many of the ships actually sailed right by Port Townsend Bay slowing only long enough to pick up or drop off the Sea Captains who build their marvelous homes on the bluffs overlooking the city. Wives of these Captains walked the Widows Walks awaiting these passing ships and a glimpse of their men being rowed ashore to the town dock after a long ocean voyages.

It was in this steaming brew of nautical history, and dreamy sensory memories that the infectious idea to actually build a boat, got hold of me. Once I was exposed, the ailment settled into all the deepest parts of my spirit: My love of the sea, adventure, working with my hands, and building things both practical and beautiful. It only raised my fever to realize I didn't know a darn thing about building a boat.

How difficult could it actually be if Welshmen were making and rowing Coracles (a wicker-work of ash covered with animal skins) thousands of years ago in the Atlantic off the coast of Wales and Ireland? "Uncivilized" people were making sailing boats long before the machine world we live in, and with fewer and more primitive tools than I had available. My Grandfather's enchanting yellow National Geographic magazines had filled my mind with reed boats of the Phoenicians and a boat named for an Inca God, called "Kon Tiki."

In a much less magisterial way than Thor Heyerdahl, I cleared a space in the single car garage of my Willamette street house in Eugene. The plans and materials list for the Yankee Tender had arrived and it was time do more than day dream over the cross sections, detailed drawings of breasthooks, transom bevels and chine. It was time to wade in to a bewildering array of terms.

Steam bending white oak, clear vertical grain western red cedar, locust, Honduras mahogany - bronze, bronze and more bronze. Square drive wood screws, slotted and Philips head screws, clinch nails, rivets and roves of copper; Jesus, was it ever exciting.

I remember one old guy taking me aside in the fasteners section of a boat chandlery one day. "Never use brass on a boat," he said, with a stern look in his eyes. "Stainless steel is even to be suspected unless you are sure about the supplier." I was awash in new terms and building principles and the hard held opinions of every salty looking guy that came along. I loved the feeling of being an insider, but I felt lost and hopeless about my ability to actually bring this plan to life.

I dreamed Noah spoke to me: “Build it one step at a time.” Begin at the beginning and cut the first board, calculate the first angle and fasten the boards together one at a time.” I learned, the hard way, to be aware of the big picture but to stay focused on short-term issues; to read ahead enough to see how “Slot A and Hole B” related one to the other, but not to get too far ahead of myself.

BUILDING A BOAT, STEP #12: BUY THE LUMBER.

Honduran or big-leaf mahogany (Swietenia macrophylla), with a range from Mexico to southern Amazonia in Brazil, the most widespread species of mahogany and the only true mahogany species commercially grown today.
WIKIPEDIA

It is a long drive to any boat lumberyard from the Willamette Valley. Turning the key and pushing the floorboard starter button on my old pickup truck was always a crapshoot. Would the engine fire up and run? Would the Battery be dead? Would the engine run but the headlights fail? The biggest worry? The old flat-head-six motor would choose this day of its 25 year life, to blow up.

A long trip at fifty-five miles an hour was a lot to ask of a 1951 Dodge Truck. The damp air of that early summer morning was kind to both the Dodge and me. Our destination was an old, north Puget Sound port city. Anacortes has served the marine industry since 1891 and the buildings and lumberyard at Flounder Bay Boat Lumber were built sometime early in those years. Some might say Anacortes was run down and old, but to me a working port town is a joy. My eyes saw working boats being built, repaired, and stored by working men and women with no time or patience for pretense.

The previous months had been filled with research about wood types, calculating the dimensions of each individual piece of wood on the boat. I had counted and categorized fasteners and sorted out how I could most efficiently use each board. I compulsively poured over the plan drawings and I finally felt ready for this buying trip.

The small chandlery of Flounder Bay was a tidy, naturally lit space with a few well-displayed tools and fasteners. I walked from it into the dark cavern of the lumber warehouse and moved from morning sun into an old, dark, two-story sanctuary of wood beams, saw dust and fresh cut wood. Piled, stacked, racked, stickered, and beautiful. I couldn't take it all in. The sensory overload was magnificent.

I hate to seem a wood geek, but I'll never forget the gigantic band saw sitting over in one corner. It stood 10 ft tall and had a table that must have been two feet on a side. The throat, where wood could be cut, was at least two feet deep. Huge steel wheels turned the two-inch wide saw blade at frightening speeds, but oh, how smoothly it could cut a wide plank out of a large piece of timber.

"So, what'a'ya need," the guy asked. My wish list, so obsessively created over many months, was neatly folded in my blue work shirt pocket. I pulled it out and started to read.

1. Clear vertical grain western red cedar, 12 inches wide by 3/8 inch thick by 12 feet long, about 90 linear ft.
2. Long, straight-grained white oak, 1 inch by 6 inches by 14 feet
3. Oak 3/4 inch thick by 6 inches wide by 8 feet long
4. Something nice for a pretty transom. Maybe Honduras Mahogany, 1x6x20
5. Bronze screws
6. Copper clinch nails

7. Pine for building the molds
8. Maybe some Black Locus for the stem, breast hook and quarter knees

To my amazement he just said o.k. and got at the task of gathering what I needed. A mysterious and overwhelming task for me was just another day at the lumberyard for him. He reminded me of my father, the mill worker. Managing complex orders of wood for him was little different from manipulating multiple aspects of Psychological theory for me. Yet, I valued his skill above my own.

It is hard to describe the collision of my fears and obsessive preparation in contrast to the warehouse man's humdrum dailiness. I wanted him to be as awe struck as I was. The intersection of our lives, mine all "gee whiz and oh my gosh," his, "is that all you need," was the first of many such perception changing encounters while building the boat. My monumental under-taking was just another small task in a busy day for him. I wanted and still want people to be impressed with my monumental undertaking. He could have cared less.

We loaded the old Dodge to the brim (or should I say gunwales), covered and tied it all down, and I was out of the yard in less than an hour on the clock with empty pockets and a full heart. For me a chasm had opened, I slipped free of time and training and earthly bounds. I walked through a curtain of time, skill, history and language and was forever changed.

Forever changed? Perhaps. In my academic world we often confused talk with action. Running a few ideas through one's mind was thought to be worthy of a day's work. In the world of boat building more was required than thinking and making long lists. It was now time to actually begin to build the boat, to make a pile of exotic lumber into a boat that stayed upright, did not leak excessively and could safely carry a passenger keeping the water out and the passenger in.

BUILDING A BOAT, STEP #13: MAKE SAWDUST NOT WORDS.

"A chine, in boating refers to a sharp angle in the hull, an intersection of the bottom and sides of a boat."

The chines on my boat are constructed from a continuous pieces of white oak running from the stem to the transom and connecting bottom to hull. One chine on either side of the bottom of the boat. A thirteen foot long, multi-angled chunk of hardwood that must be steam bent to form the shape of the boat's bottom and accommodate many bronze fasteners from outside as well as inside the hull. The beautifully curving lines of the Yankee Tender were what attracted me to the boat from the beginning. The elegant, compound curves that define this craft from stem to stern, top to bottom, start with the chine.

The primary challenge of attaching a chine is to bend the long piece of hardwood over a framework created of scrap wood that is upside-down, creating a reversed shell of the boat's hull. Imagine, if you will, bending a long piece of dry pasta over a half shell of an eggplant. Narrow at one end, broad at the other. Robust full curves connecting the ends. Now, make the eggplant 13 feet long and nearly 3 feet deep. As you know, wood can be supple, can bend and has some flexibility; however, bending wood of this length and dimension seriously challenged my rules of what was possible in the physical world.

The solution? Steam bending. It turns out that the cellular structure of wood, when heated and made moist by steam, becomes quite supple and malleable. Not like spaghetti, but like a willow switch. The challenge of attaching the chine is to achieve a level of flexibility that allows it to bend in a compound curve and not break under the stress of the bend.

In my case, the bending had to be done without mechanical or machine support and all by myself. These limitations were not wise, particularly, but they were what I had available given my stubborn insistence on doing things by myself.

The first step of making the chine required me to cut one of the longest and thickest pieces of oak hauled back from Anacortes. It was a pricy board and I didn't want to waste it by breaking it or cutting it badly. The second step involved using my table saw to make the correct cuts necessary to form the sharp angle where flat bottom met the gracefully flaring sides of the boat. My workspace was so small that I had placed my table saw outside under the carport in order to have space for the boat inside and out of the weather. Shop-space, tools, and priorities were a constant problem for me. Was I to leave the boat or the saw out under the carport in the wet rainy weather?

Cutting precise angles over a long length of board is not terribly difficult but it is easy to hurry the process and cause imperfections along the length of the cut. I succeeded at the first try and took a moment to breathe. I now turned to the bending process. The challenge here was to have a continuous and stable source of wet heat. Real boat shops have steam boxes built especially for this job, but I didn't have one. In fact, I was working in my garage, a space barely big enough for a small car. I had to place the boat frame from corner to corner. Only inches remained at either end of the boat to maneuver, and little more that a few feet on either side remained for all of this bending and steaming.

My plan was to attach the transom end of the chine with the appropriate bronze screw and a clamp, just to be sure it would hold. At this point in the process, the chine stuck up in the air at a weirdly jaunty angle, nearly touching the garage roof. I wrapped the chine in old rags, towels, and parts of rug and poured boiling water over its length. I kept it hot by adding more hot water over the next 10 minutes. The water made a godawful mess on the floor of the garage but I forged ahead. Testing the flexibility of the wood after the last pouring of hot water I began a slow but deliberate bending of this 14-foot board along the frame and towards the bow-stem. I'd added an extra foot to the chine's length. Coming up an inch short was not an option in this operation. I could always cut off the excess later.

At first the bending went easily from frame to frame along the length of the boat. As I neared the transom the curve tightened and the flexibility came out of the wood. I began to realize the jeopardy I was in. If one end of the board broke free under the strain, or if my hands slipped off the hot, sharp edged board it could take my head off. Sweating, wet with hot water and straining to make the last foot of bend come home I was overcome with the thought of an unseen flaw in the wood. A small-unnoticed knot in the center of the board that might snap at any moment. It was likely that I would be killed or seriously hurt if this thing came loose from its moorings or broke apart. Stopping was not an option, so I pushed on nearly at the end of my strength and nearly at the bow end of the board. "Now," I said to myself. "Hold strong and steady and screw the thing home, and let's hope the damn screw holds."

Compound bevels, complex curves, extraordinary tension and no back up, no experience to call on. No wonder I liked the project, it pushed me in real and unpredictable ways. I was scared plenty and pleased even more when the screw held, the board didn't shatter and one of the two chines was home. Now for the second one.

Aside from the thwarts (seats for you land lubbers), there are no square boards in the whole boat. As one gracefully curving piece of wood mates with another, the complexity of the fitted pieces become ever more complex. The lessons of one step did not directly mean increased skills to succeed at the next step. As the angles and joints became more complex I learned to make practice models of a joint using cheap scrap wood. It saved me innumerable amounts of expensive wood and allowed me to make the big errors on a practice piece rather than the real boat. I navigated the building of the boat one waypoint at a time, using my navigational skills and the faith that a homeport awaited me when the long voyage was over.

BUILDING A BOAT, STEP #14: PLAN FOR UNEXPECTED DISTRACTIONS AND THEN PLAN FOR MORE UNEXPECTED DISTRACTIONS.

Plank: The boards which form the hull of a wooden boat.
SEA TALK NAUTICAL DICTIONARY

Somewhere between laying on the last cedar plank of the hull and the end of my first marriage, my work on the boat stalled in the maelstrom of major life transitions. In short: I lost custody of my garage in the divorce. I rented a small garage space, but it was not at all close to where I was living. As my life filled with complexity so did the challenge of driving the distance to the boat shop.

Relationship changes caused me to find a new place to live. I rented a small apartment on the edge of the working waterfront of Everett, Washington. Staring out over the harbor became my main entertainment on quiet evenings alone. As always the tidewater ebbing and flowing before me settled my soul. I thought again of living nearer the water and found myself searching for property on a small island nearby. Whidbey Island offered salt water views at a price I could afford and a community of people as weird as I had become. I found a small piece of property with a rundown cabin perched on a high bluff looking over Useless Bay and Admiralty Inlet.

As ever, I continued to work on the boat. Turned right side up and with the hull planking complete and the inner stem and transom in place, she began to look like a real boat. I was full of pride but the boat had very little strength or stability without interior frames. The remedy, according to the much trusted plans was to “get out the frames.” I had plan drawings and materials guidelines, but the instructions only said, frustratingly, “get out the frames.” I didn’t have a clue what this meant in practical terms. As I attempted to “get out the frames,” I wrongly cut oak board after oak board.

Each frame was two feet long and one inch wide. It was to be screwed to the now infamous chines and tapered up to the top of the hull, at a plank known as a sheer plank. I need 22 frames in all but I’ll be damned if I couldn’t get but one or two of them to fit properly. Demoralized, I gave up. The boat sat for months. The ever-increasing complexity of the boat building skills required, the complexity of my relationships and work commitments caused a crisis of priorities. I must concede as the cedar hull and bottom neared completion I couldn’t move forward on the project. I just didn’t have the skill necessary.

It was in these months of change, confusion, and uncertainty that I moved in with the person who would become my second wife. She had a house perched on the edge of the Pilchuck River in the foothills of the Cascade Mountains, near a town called Granite Falls. The setting was beautiful but I was farther away from the sea than I’d been since leaving the cursed Oregon valley. I abandoned the offer to buy the house on Whidbey Island and moved the boat to a drafty but lovely shop space at my new home.

Beautiful as it was, the Granite Falls house was a handyman’s dream, or nightmare, depending on one’s state of mind. The handyman in me could see endless opportunities to express my interest in carpentry and home repair. To illustrate how bad it was, the water in the toilet bowel froze solid on cold winter nights. Mold grew in the wet corners where the fireplace chimney went through the roof and a perfectly good furnace was not functioning because a previous lover of my partner had pulled out all of the furnace ductwork for reasons known only to him.

Of necessity, the house repairs took precedent in money, time and skill over everything, including the boat project. I needed time and more space in the shop for the ever-expanding projects.

I rigged a set of pulleys and ropes to the high ceiling of the shop and hoisted the Yankee Tender up into the peak of the A frame shop. Sadly, she hung there for the fifteen-year duration of my second marriage and the never-ending string of renovation projects. The bad news? The boat became a bird's nest and sometimes water catcher from regular leaks in the old cedar shake roof. The boat planes faded and pieces were lost. Some of my precious boat lumber was lost, used for other projects or jammed into shop corners. The good news? My wood working skills and patience increased as I gathered ever more sophisticated project experience and ever better wood working tools.

During this long middle passage of my life both the boat and my vagabond seafaring life hung on the rafters in much the same way. I stopped orienting to the sea and moved to the mountains. I led a high country river life and my professional life made an academic and intellectual course change. I don't mean to say I did no traveling, but Masefield's poem found its way off the wall of my office and into the back of a desk drawer. I further buried the Navy years and stopped day dreaming about tugboats and sailing.

In fact I travelled to Europe, Mexico, Japan, Florida and California in those years. I worked long hours at teaching and higher education and explored different social realms of the world. Building took on more pedestrian forms as I added on to the house, creating bedrooms and bookshelves.

Then, on a May morning in 1995, as the sun rose from behind Mt. Pilchuck, I found myself ship-wrecked by the unexpected death of my wife. Her death brought into question all I had thought central in my life. The house, my work, life itself lost a sense of direction. Any notions about life purpose, goals and continuity were brought into question or buried in grief.

One wet fall evening, in that first winter of loss, I rented the Disney classic, Snow White and the Seven Dwarfs. Broiling two pork chops and baking some tater-tots I settled in to my comfy chair anticipating a nostalgic trip back to simpler times and my dinner tray sat softly lighted by the TV screen.

"Hi ho, hi ho, it's off to work we go."

The seven dwarfs found their simple working lives turned over by the arrival of Snow White. Why was it I had never noticed the implications this story had for men and women and relationships? I sat in the half-light of the TV screen, dumbstruck by the ways this movie mirrored my life with women. The absence of a constant, the missing magnetic pull of "woman" had allowed me to rethink my life with women. Living alone I understood how household projects, maintenance, remodeling, and simple cleaning chores could lose all meaning. The cobwebs and the dust that had settled on my shop, tools and will to work with my hands began to make sense. My raison d'être for much of my life was a changing but ever-present Snow White of one sort or another. Mom, Michele, Mimi, all of the "M" women of my life. Watching this movie classic I wondered who would coo an adoring appreciation for my work now? Is it possible John Masefield's wayfaring men went "down to the sea again" because it made their women coo? I doubt it, but I was a long time reconsidering my need for the approval of women and the role their approval played in motivating my behavior.

Many books are written about sailors washed up on some god-forsaken shore and lost for some hazy period of time. The plot of these stories often hinge on the power of unforeseen events to awaken them to a new life; and so it was with me. I awakened to a new life with the serendipitous meeting of a mature, independent and strong mother of three adult children. Her name didn't start with the letter M; it was Susan. We were two fifty something adults with lots of life behind us who had found their way into a truly wonderful relationship.

BUILDING A BOAT, STEP #15: THE MAN WHO BEGINS TO BUILD A BOAT MAY NOT BE THE MAN WHO WILL FINISH IT.

"Life is what happens while you are busy making other plans."
JOHN LENNON

The spring of 2012 was wet and slow to break winter's miserable grip on my workshop. Last summers firewood was nearly gone and a hot fire in the shop stove barely kept the damp cold out of my hands. My grandson Samuel and I were making wooden swords and shields for a planned battle royal with some of his friends. He and I had worked together in my shop since he was big enough to hold a hammer and drive a nail. Scrap boards, duct tape, and imagination kept us busy. Pointing to the peak of the shop ceiling he said, "Grampa, what is that thing hanging up there?" "A boat I've been building for a long time," I said. He considered it, his eyes focusing on the sawdust covered floor. "Why don't you bring it down and work on it?" Many others had asked that question through the years but none of them had looked at me with the unassuming, genuinely curious, brown eyes of an adolescent boy that I had come to respect and love. Since he was a small boy he had asked me questions and I had tried to always answer them with honesty and forthrightness. I'll never forget his look, when at nine years old, he asked if I had killed anyone during the war. Then as now, his questions did not have simple answers and his young mind struggled to comprehend my nuanced, rambling answers.

Essentially, this story is my answer to Sam about why the boat was on the ceiling, and how it had come to exist at all, but on that wet spring day we agreed that it was time to make space for the boat on the shop floor and that he would help me work on it if I brought it down from the ceiling.

As you already know, the boat took the place of pride between the chop saw and the table saw and was close enough to feel the fire's warmth from the shop stove. I began to clean off the bird droppings, water stains and to throw away the skeletal remains of two birds unlucky enough to have become caught inside the hull of the boat. Each week as Sam came to visit, and before we once more turned the shop into a weapons armory, I would show him what I had done during the week. In the early weeks it was a set of replacement plans, later I asked him to help me sort out the intricacies of cutting the oak frames that had been my demise years earlier and finally I would ask for his help on some small task on the boat each week. Cross bows, shoulder guards and more swords would follow.

The glorious July day when I finally "got out" the last of twenty-two oak frames, a wave of pride and relief flooded over me. It was a solitary moment. As I called Susan out to show her, she made appropriate cooing sounds and then said dinner would be ready in about 20 minutes. An uncomfortably familiar feeling came over me when I accepted that no other person in the world could fully appreciate the importance of this moment. As the small gathering of Paul's in my head, the young war

vet, the mid-life professional, the grieving man, and the retired senior citizen toasted a make believe glass of champagne over the hull of the Yankee Tender, I knew I would finish this project. We all knew we would finish this 12 1/2 foot dream and row it proudly into some forgotten cove as waves broke against the bow.

BUILDING A BOAT, STEP #16: DON'T FORGET THE PROPULSION SYSTEM.

"Oar n. An implement for impelling a boat, being a slender piece of timber, usually ash or spruce, with a grip or handle at one end and a broad blade at the other. The part which rests in the rowlock is called the loom."
COLLABORATIVE INTERNATIONAL DICTIONARY OF ENGLISH

The finishing of the boat required one last drive to a lumberyard. After some shopping for oars I realized I could build my own oars with the help of a set of plans. Wouldn't you know that this would require a search for a 12-foot chunk of Sitka Spruce? After much calling around and a failed attempt to have a plank delivered to my house, an old boat guy told me the McClanahan Lumber Company in Forks, Washington, would have what I needed. A brief phone call later I felt giddy at the thought of a long days drive past Port Townsend and around the tip of the state to a beautiful wild stretch of the northwest coast of Washington.

The mill was a classic and reminded me of the small sawmill my father and uncle had tried to make money with when I was a child. Needless to say I was in love with McClanahans mill long before my feet shuffle-stepped around deep mud puddles and odds and ends of logs. Larry McClanahan greeted me in the mill yard and offered a firm handshake. I reminded him what I wanted and of course he remembered. I followed him to a large two story, steel roofed storage building. We cut through the middle of the mill up and over the log carriage, around the massive band saw, our boots kicking sawdust and wood scraps as we went. The mill itself wasn't running but an old guy nodded his head at me from beneath the green chain where he greased fittings in preparation for more sawing.

As I walked into the non-descript, metal roofed storage building, my breath caught for a moment. Stacks of lumber, not unlike my first experience at Flounder Bay Boat Lumber decades before, glowed out at me. Without looking, Larry pointed behind him and half way up a two story high pile of white, rough sawn boards. He said, "I think that piece of spruce up there will be exactly what you are looking for." He fired up the forklift and after moving piles of lumber he delivered the promised board to my feet. It was sheer beauty. A long white piece of clear-grained Sitka Spruce. He helped me load it on top of my car and I turned around to retrace the steps of the five-hour, two ferry boat trip. This time with a big smile on my face and a perfect chunk of wood singing in the roof rack ropes as I drove home.

The oar project finished, I sat about finding a trailer to take the Yankee Tender to the place of her sea trials. It was surprisingly difficult to find a used trailer and in the end I broke down and bought a new one. What's another thousand dollars at this point in the story?

The very real possibility that the boat would leak like a sieve caused a cold sweat to break out on my back. Though it wasn't like she would sink outright, my mind ran wild with catastrophic possibilities. As much as I wanted to keep my humiliation a private matter and take the boat out alone for her first launch, my good sense got the best of me.

Memorial Day dawned sunny and calm, a perfect day to finally put my lifetime project to the real test. I had a few unexpected last minute challenges. I found myself sitting in the car with a jack-knifed boat trailer in the middle of a small boat launch. Some grand and magnanimous god of boat builders and fools had blessed me with an empty launch and not another soul to witness my humiliation. I tried again and again to line the trailer up with the narrow uneven boat ramp and eventually, after proving I really could cuss like a sailor, I had the Yankee Tender in the water.

She floated with perfect trim and rowed like a dream. She moved through the water straight and true leaving a small wake astern as the oars spun mini-whirlpools in the water with each stroke of the oars.

BUILDING A BOAT, STEP #17: WHEN THE LONG TRICK'S OVER.

"He knew now that it was his own will to happiness which must make the next move. But if he was to do so, he realized that he must come to terms with time, that to have time was at once the most magnificent and the most dangerous of experiments. Idleness is fatal only to the mediocre."
— ALBERT CAMUS, *A HAPPY DEATH*

Now, with the boat finished, the time and freedom created by my retirement caused long considered but unfinished plans to surface for Susan and I. For years we had talked about our need to simplify our lives, downsize our life style, and find a new home that would facilitate both. Even though we loved living on the edge of the river, surrounded by 150 year old fir trees, we had become restless and ready to enjoy new adventures in a new place. Reopening the boat project had rekindled my infatuation with tidal water and open sky. And my need to leave the ghosts and complexity of the Granite Falls house nagged me to reclaim some old dreams. But first, my old dreams needed to dovetail with the dreams held near to Susan's heart.

Months of exploring and considering the boggling array of beautiful places to live on North Puget Sound overwhelmed us. Feeling lost, we gave up the search for a new home. It took a quiet New Years in an elegant old Seattle Hotel to create the time for us to sit quietly and carefully listen to what was in our hearts. The insistent optimism of a New Year's Eve helped us distill or cook down the ingredients of our uncertainty. We finally came to a shared idea of what we were looking for in these late years. The words "peaceful" and "serene" became our new watchwords. We wanted a new home in a new location that was close enough to children and grandchildren, but more over would be peaceful and serene. We finally allowed that our souls would know the place when we found it. After two months of reinvigorated searching, a house on Whidbey Island found us.

One day, visiting friends on the island, we noticed the people across the street cleaning out their garage. These neighbors, we were told, rarely visited their summer house. Curiosity sparked an urge to go over and ask if they were preparing to sell the house. It seemed bold and a bit rambunctious but the neighbors surprising and affirmative response was equally amazing. Could it be, that after so much searching and wondering and rejecting houses and locations we could just stumble onto our peaceful and serene new home? Certainly, isn't that the way it is supposed to happen in this kind of tale?

Four seasons, a full year, have passed. The open western sky and brilliant sunsets over Puget Sound and the Olympic mountains cause us to stop, stare and sigh to each other on a regular basis. The realization that we have moved just a few miles from the island house I didn't buy all of those years ago when my life veered off course and into the mountain once more illustrates the unpredictability, and the inevitability of life.

Many lake and salt-water boat trips have bolstered my faith in the seaworthiness of my little tender. Taking the boat out crabbing on the tidewaters of Puget Sound, in rain, wind and sun, has tested my rowing skills and Sam's resolve. He seems impressed that she actually floats and after catching our first fresh crabs and eating them he is more

excited then ever that we have taken that old derelict off of the ceiling of my shop.

Could I ever have imagined this story? The boat navigating its way through so many crosscurrents and back-eddies has found her way home to the sea after all.

One late summer afternoon Susan's middle son Joshua and I were admiring the boat. He asked me what I was to do with it now that it was done. Without much of a thought I said, "I don't know. I've always been more focused on building a boat than on having one. I guess I don't really care what happens with it." His perplexed look made me smile inside.

Pulling the oars of the Yankee tender with a full sweep into a stiff breeze, my shoulders let out a small moan. As satisfying as a row boat can be, it seems reasonable to take advantage of the wind to give my body a rest, and besides, wouldn't it be fun to *sail* a small boat. All I need is a mast, leeboard and rudder and she'll sail like a dream. She is not intended to be a sailboat, but it seems an alternative power source would be nice (picture a sly smile on my face as you read this passage). I just happened to possess a lovely Sitka Spruce board left over from McClanahans lumber mill that just calls out to be turned into a stout mast able to hold a nice little spritsail.

Now, due to the realities of island life, I regularly find myself standing on the deck of a ferryboat transporting me to and from the mainland. The large Diesel engines thrum up through my feet. The wind, blowing in my face during these crossings, smells of salt. From my perch on the upper deck the seagulls fly so close I can reach out and feed them. As I look past them through the waning light to my new home my eye is caught by the red and green navigation lights of a tugboat running southward to Seattle. The three white lights shining in her mast tell me she is a working tug with a large tow, running ahead of the tide and bound for her own safe harbor.

The sea, the wind, the fog shrouded beaches, fill me with certainty. I have returned to where I was intended to be so many years ago. The quiet joy of returning to this place fills me in a way not felt since returning home from the war. I move easily across the steel ferry deck. My obligation is complete, my service fulfilled, my fear rests quietly off at the edges of my soul.

A big sea swell pushes against the hull of the ferry causing a deep primal shudder. It isn't like a punch, not a slap, but it is a deep realization in my body that this 4000 ton vessel has been lifted without effort and moved with certainty to where the water wanted to take it. No anger, no will, just raw force acting without malice or even intent; the motion is more akin to fate or divine intention. Though I struggle to name it, this story has been filled with examples of the immutable force I'm trying to describe.

A smile curves the corners of my mouth as I think of the double meaning of the words *tug* and *pull* and *draft.* My life has been moved by the forces I've danced with as I pull the oars of my boat and dream tugboat dreams. The nightmares of our nations draft took me from my life once and now I find the tug of retirement moves me in unexpected ways as I'm pulled up on the beach to the love of a grandson and a future with my soulful lover and partner.

Standing on the deck of my house looking out across Useless Bay, I hear a foghorn at Point No Point in the distance. Just for a moment I would swear it is the deep resonant voice of Mr. Stefon.

"and all I ask is a
merry yarn from a
laughing fellow rover
and quiet sleep and a
sweet dream when the
long trick's over."

47645372R00038

Made in the USA
Charleston, SC
12 October 2015